Sister Emmanuel

The Beautiful Story of Medjugorje
as Told to Children
from 7 to 97 years of age

children
of
Medjugorje

The author does not intend to preempt the judgment of the Church with regard to private revelations, but only to inform the readers about facts happening in Medjugorje and the alleged apparitions, starting on June 24, 1981.

The Beautiful Story of Medjugorje
As Told to Children from 7 to 97 years of age

Gaby - Sr Emmanuel - Chrissey - Rosie

© Children of Medjugorje Inc, 2013
Translated from French by Anne Laboe
Graphic design: Nancy Cleland, USA
Drawings: Pascale Nouailhat, France, 2012
Photos: © Bernard Gallagher, UK, and private archives

This book is also available as a E-Book

For Distribution, see www.childrenofmedjugorje.com
comments@childrenofmedjugorje.com

Versions in French (original), Italian, Portuguese, Spanish, Polish, German, Dutch, Chinese, Slovenian, Arabic, Croatian, Korean, Indonesian, slovakian: See www.childrenofmedjugorje.com

Printer: Grafotisak, BiH, August 2013 - www.grafotisak.com

First, I want to thank you for having chosen this book! You'll see, you won't be disappointed by the story that I'm going to tell you: the beautiful story of Medjugorje! A unique, fascinating, marvelous story! A true story!

1. Other Apparitions in the World

Before beginning this story, I'd like to say a few words about other places where the Blessed Virgin Mary has appeared in the world. It's important for you to be familiar with them, too. I'm sure you know about Lourdes! There is also Fatima, in Portugal; Guadalupe, in Mexico; Baneux, in Belgium; Notre-Dame du Laus, in the French Alps; Knock, in Ireland, and so many, many others.

And you see, in each place where there is an apparition, the Blessed Mother comes with a very specific goal. She has a plan. Since she is a mother, she always comes to do something good for her children; that's her plan. She loves us so much! She wants to help us become better; she wants to console us in our troubles; she wants to talk to us about Jesus; she helps us to love Him more and more; she teaches us; she invites us to live as God would like us to live. In short, whenever our Mother comes from heaven to earth, she brings with her great gifts for us all.

Let me give you a few examples:

When Mary appeared to Saint Catherine Labouré, at the "Rue du Bac" in Paris, do you know what she gave her? Think about it . . . it was the Miraculous Medal!

And there on the Rue du Bac, Mary asked us to wear that medal as a sign that we have put ourselves under her motherly protection. And how many miracles of protection have taken place thanks to that medal!

Another example is when Our Lady came to Juan Diego in Guadalupe, which is in Mexico. Because of her apparitions and her beautiful messages, thousands and thousands of Aztecs were baptized and became Christian, even though they did not know Jesus! Our Lady brought Jesus to the people of Mexico.

And in Lourdes: Have you seen pictures of all the sick people who go there? It's amazing! Mary waits for them, to console them, to comfort them, and sometimes even to cure them. She brought healing to the people of France.

And, in Fatima, in Portugal, Mary asked three little shepherd children to pray the rosary and to make little sacrifices. Well, thanks to those prayers, a terrible war, the First World War, was stopped. Mary brought peace.

Oh, I forgot! There's a very beautiful story from Italy, when Mary appeared to Bruno Cornacchiola and his three children, in Rome (at a place called "The Three Fountains"). What a wonderful story as well! This Bruno was a criminal. He wanted to kill Pope Pius XII with a knife, but after having seen the Blessed Mother, he changed completely. He even went to Rome to give his knife to the Pope and to ask him for forgiveness for his plan. You see how the Blessed Mother did him good! She brought him reconciliation!

And she brings all of these gifts to us too.

Have you noticed that often Mary chooses children to transmit messages? And especially poor children? Why is that?

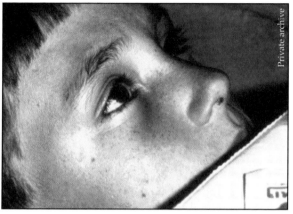

The visionary Jakov in ectasy (1982)

Jesus gives us the answer. He said, "Blessed are the pure of heart, for they shall see God." A child has a purer heart than we adults do, because a child has sinned less. His little heart is still new, since it came fresh from the hands of the Creator! Often, Mary chooses young shepherds as well, because they live outside, in nature, and are closer to creation and to the Creator. They lead a simple life. They aren't distracted or warped by all that is said on television or the internet. Their souls are fresher. They know how to look at the stars, listen to the wind blow, and watch the seasons go by.

2. Presentation on the Apparitions of Medjugorje

So, back to the story at hand. One day, the Blessed Mother decided to appear in Yugoslavia, in a country now called Bosnia & Herzegovina. Where is that? Do you see the country that looks like a boot? That's Italy! From Italy, you cross the Adriatic Sea to Croatia, go a little further inland and you come to Bosnia & Herzegovina and Medjugorje. You weren't even born when the Blessed Mother came to that little village in 1981. That day was a big Feast day, the Feast of St. John the Baptist! Do you remember him? You've heard about him in the Bible. He's the cousin

of Jesus, the one who preached in the desert to prepare the way for Jesus.

On that day, a group of children and teenagers, decided to meet each other for a walk. Two girls left first and arrived at the foot of the little hill that overlooked their village. Their names were Ivanka and Mirjana. They were 16 years old. They were chatting with one another about this and that, you know, the way girls do.

Suddenly, Ivanka saw on the hill a beautiful lady, a very beautiful lady, who didn't look like the women in her village. She was dressed in a long robe, full of light. In her arms, she carried a tiny baby whom she was covering and uncovering with a light cloth, as if to show him to Ivanka. She was waving with her hand towards Ivanka. Ivanka couldn't believe her eyes! You can imagine the shock! She had never heard about other apparitions like Lourdes or Fatima. She didn't even know that Mary could appear on earth! She was so astonished that she fell to her knees! She couldn't take her eyes off this lady. Then she called out to her friend Mirjana and said to her, "Look, Mirjana, there's Gospa! ("Gospa" is the name of Our Lady in Croatian). Look how beautiful she is!" No wonder Mirjana made fun of her, saying something like, "But Ivanka, what are you talking about! You don't really believe that the Mother of God would come to see us, do you? Are you crazy?"

But, surprisingly, she felt her head being turned towards the hillside, and guess what she saw? The same thing as Ivanka saw! The beautiful Lady was really there and Mirjana had the same reaction as Ivanka: at the shock, she fell to her knees, struck dumb with surprise, fear, and joy all mixed up together.

The two girls stayed like that for quite a while, looking at this strange and splendid Lady. The Lady smiled at them and gestured to them to come towards her. But the two girls' feet were glued to the ground. They didn't dare move! It was then that Vicka, a young girl of 17, came to join them on their walk. She found her friends kneeling on the side of the road, their eyes staring at the hill, and she

Five of the visionaries on Apparition Hill in 1982

began to make fun of them and pestered them to get up. "What are you doing down on your knees at the side of the road? That's no place to pray!" But they said, "Look Vicka! Look on the hill, there is Gospa!" But Vicka didn't even look up. She took off her shoes and began to run away.

On her way, she met Ivan, who was just walking back to watch some basketball game on his friend's television. Vicka said to him, "Quick, come with me to join the other girls, something strange is happening!" Vicka arrived with Ivan at the place where the two girls were on their knees, and soon Ivan also saw Our Lady. What a shock! He was so afraid that he ran away too. The poor boy couldn't sleep that night, as he kept saying to himself, "Is it really Our Lady? What shall I do if she appears in my room? How shall I get down from the first floor?!"

As for Vicka, she stayed with Ivanka and Mirjana at the foot of the hill. Then it was as if someone turned her head aside and she too saw the Lady. She was so startled! She exclaimed, "Oh, you are right!! How beautiful she is!" Afterwards, on their way home, they went to their neighbor's house. When the girls entered the house, they could not help but blurt out excitedly that they had seen Our Lady on the hill. But the reaction of the people there was astonishing; the girls were accused of lying.

That day, six young people from the village saw Our Lady, and all of them saw her the same way. I bet you'd also like to know how Mary looked, wouldn't you?

The visionary Vicka Ivanković in 1982

3. What does Mary look like?

First, she sent three flashes of light before she came. As soon as she was there, the visionaries fell to their knees, and you could see their faces, their eyes filled up with light. They said it was impossible to describe the beauty of Our Lady. She was too, too beautiful! She looked to be about 18, but the visionaries say that it is difficult to guess her age. The children were so filled with happiness and awe that they would have liked to stay with her forever. She had long, black hair, blue eyes and a beautiful complexion. On her head was a crown with 12 stars which illuminated the whole hill. The stars were not connected to one another, it was as if they were floating above the Lady's head in a harmonious way. Our Lady wore a white veil, a grey-blue robe, a color that doesn't exist on earth. Her feet were hidden by a swirling white cloud.

Private archive

The six visionaries during an apparition of Our Lady in 1982

Mary's image as described by the seers

© Enfants de Medjugorje 1994

4. The Christians were in a difficult situation in Medjugorje

At this point, I have to explain something that will help you understand the rest of the story.

At this particular time, the whole village was greatly suffering because there was an atheist government in charge of all of Yugoslavia. What's that, you ask. Well a government is a body of people who make laws to help people live together safely. But an atheist government says that God does not exist. In fact, those in the government would have liked it if no one believed in God ever again, so some even made laws against believing in God or practicing their faith. Sometimes they even threatened the Christians with prison if they gathered to pray or to do anything related to God.

So, you can imagine the problem for these six children and for their families: how could they explain that they saw the Mother of Jesus to people who didn't believe in Jesus or Mary, or in anything supernatural, and who thought that after death, there is nothing, no heaven, no hell, nothing. It was terrible!

So everyone paid close attention to the "Militia" guards. But that evening, after the visionaries returned home, can you guess what happened?

Within a few hours, the whole village knew! At the time, however, these very poor families didn't even have telephones in their homes, or cells phones, MP3 players, video games or other electronics that you are familiar with today. They didn't even know such things existed! But they had a way of communicating that was even nicer than all those gadgets: they talked to each other, they visited each other and they shared things around the table. They all knew one another. The atmosphere was very warm in their homes. Families were large, so you could see many children around playing inside and out. Houses overflowed with life, they were indeed busy places!

Saint James's church at the beginning of the apparitions

5. The next day and following...

On June 25, the children felt an urge to go back to the same place. Now let me tell you their names: First Vicka, who was 17, then there was Ivan, Marija, Ivanka, and Mirjana, all aged 16. Then little Jakov, who was 10.

The six seers, Ivan, Marija, Ivanka, Mirjana Jakov and Vicka in 1982

That day, the children gathered at the foot of the hill, hoping that the Lady would come again. They felt excitement and fear at the same time. She did come, smiling and joyful, but without the baby. She was floating on a cloud, like the day before. She signaled for them to come towards her. They felt such a motherly love that their fears disappeared. Ivanka asked her,

"Where is my mother?" The Lady smiled and said, "Your mother is with me!"

She spoke in Croatian, but the way she speaks is slower than ours. Her voice is like a melody, like music.

On the 3rd day Mary invited the visionaries again to join her on the hill. They arrived at the top of the hill so quickly that everyone who was there waiting couldn't believe it. It was as if they were carried up and over the rocks and thorns to the top, without being hurt. They had no idea that this was only the beginning of a long series of marvelous deeds that Our Lady would let them experience for years, and that would change the life of their little village.

The elders were very cautious and wise. Vicka's grandmother said to her, "Satan can disguise himself as a beautiful person to attract your attention and then he reveals himself to you. Here, take this holy water with you! If the lady comes back, sprinkle her with it. If she comes from God, she'll stay, but if she doesn't come from God, she'll disappear." What a clever grandmother!

Once on the hill, Mirjana asked the Lady, "Who are you?" Then Vicka remembered the holy water that her grandmother had given her in order to test the person who was appearing. So she took the bottle and threw holy water on the Lady. The Lady smiled and said, "Don't be afraid, it's me!" It is then when she revealed who she was, "I am the Blessed Virgin Mary," she said. The more holy water Vicka threw on her, the more she smiled.

Ivanka asked her, "Why did you come here, and what do you want from us?" She said, "I came because here

I found true believers." Later on she said, "I have come to convert the whole world and to reconcile it with God. I have come to call the world to conversion for the last time."

Marija was returning home, running down the old shepherd's path, and suddenly she saw the Lady who told her, "Peace, peace, peace! Make peace with God and among yourselves. In order to do that, one has to believe, pray, fast, and go to confession."

The visionaries thought everyone could see her. Everything was so new to them! They had no idea they were the only six who would ever see her. Such was God's plan. And you know what the great surprise was for them? From that day on, Our Lady has come every day to see them, every day I tell you! Still today, she comes to Ivan, Marija, and Vicka. What does she do with them?

At the time, the visionaries were still young and inexperienced, so she did what any mother would do, she explained everything to them: how to live with Jesus, how to pray with the heart, how to work well, how to behave in the family, how to help the poor or the sick, how to make peace with enemies, and, of course, she prayed a lot with them. Each day she spoke to them and reassured them with her immense love, because as visionaries, they had a hard time being understood. She called them "my sweet angels."

As you might expect, the "Militia" got very angry. One of them was posted in front of their door with a gun, to prevent them from going out and from sharing Mary's messages with the people. But the children were not afraid!

How could they be afraid when they could see the Mother of God every day and feel her deep love? Vicka was so brave! Since she didn't have the right to leave her house, she climbed out onto her balcony and shouted the messages at the top of her lungs, so that the whole world could hear them.

Vicka proclaims the messages from her balcony

5 bis Flames above the mountain!

God sometimes – but not often – gives visible signs to the world, signs that are completely out of the ordinary. For example, at Fatima, God gave a great sign: 70,000 people saw the sun dancing and pulsating at the last apparition of the Blessed Virgin to three little shepherds, Jacinta, Francisco, and Lucia, on October 13, 1917. But let's get back to Medjugorje. It was July, 1981. Some villagers were standing near the church with their pastor, Father Jozo, when suddenly they saw letters of fire appear in the sky right at the top of Mount Krizevac. These letters formed the word MIR, which means PEACE in Croatian. Everyone who was working

The famous cross of Mt Križevac erected in 1933 to protect the village from devastating hailstorms

outside could see this word written in the sky. You can imagine their surprise! They gestured to one another, pointing to the phenomenon, and all observed this marvel, believers and unbelievers, young and old, Catholics, Orthodox, Muslims, even the "Militia" guards. Yes, every eye was fixed on the sky. People were mute with amazement. The word MIR remained for more than ten minutes in the clear blue sky, it came over the church of St. James and it burned brilliantly!

On August 6, 1981, the Blessed Mother presented herself to the visionaries as the Queen of Peace, so you can understand that her number one concern is that all her children receive this peace in their hearts! She knows only too well how painful it is for us to have empty hearts, agitated, frustrated and full of negative emotions. She came to Medjugorje to help us break free from that situation, because her own heart contains nothing but light and love, and she wants to share with us all that she has. That's normal, she is a mom! Her desire and her goal is that our hearts should be filled, and filled with what? With whom? I see that you are already guessing: with God, of course!

That day, in Medjugorje, many of those who had not believed the testimony of the visionaries, began to question themselves. These letters of fire penetrated people's hearts, they resonated and reached out to each person. No one could remain indifferent. How could anyone deny that something very special was happening in the village? It was crystal clear: God wanted peace between everyone! And Mary was coming to tell us how to receive this peace from God in prayer, and live it among ourselves.

6. A Visit to Heaven, Purgatory, and Hell

During the first year of the apparitions, Our Lady did something very astonishing. It was summer, around one o'clock in the afternoon. Vicka and Jakov arrived at the home of Jakov's mother. It was a small, very poor house, and they said, "We're hungry, can you make us something to eat?" Jakov's mom prepared two plates for them, but when she turned around to give them to the youngsters, Vicka and Jakov had completely disappeared! As you can imagine, she was totally shocked, really panicking! She asked everyone in the area, but no one had seen the children.

So what had happened? While Jakov's mom prepared the food, the Blessed Mother appeared to the two children, unexpectedly. She asked them to take a very special journey. As a matter of fact, she invited them to come with her to see heaven, purgatory, and hell. Do you realize what I'm saying? It's unbelievable!

Local house in 1984

Jakov, who was still very young and an only child, was afraid of never returning from that long journey. He was also afraid that he might die! So he

21

answered, "Take Vicka instead. She has 8 brothers and sisters. Me, I'm all alone with my mother." Then he said, "Ladies first!"

As for Vicka, who had her feet firmly planted on the ground, she asked what time they were going to return from this strange expedition, because she had to work in the tobacco fields (all the families of the village at that time harvested tobacco in their fields, and sold it to make a little money). In any case, Our Lady quickly convinced Vicka and Jakov to go with her. When Vicka told me what happened next, I was hanging on her every word. Do you want to know too?

Heaven. Here's what Vicka told me, "The Gospa took Jakov with her right hand and me with her left hand. The ceiling of the house opened and we found ourselves in heaven." I asked her, "What's heaven like?" "We saw a very large place. It was huge, with no limits, and there was a light there that doesn't exist on earth. It was full, full of people. They were so happy, they were walking, praying, singing and the little angels were flying around. They were all very beautiful. There were no blind, no lame, nor fat or skinny people." (I even asked Vicka, 'if someone had only one leg on earth, I guess he will have two legs in heaven!'). They were all around 30 years old. They were dressed in long robes of different colors, colors that don't exist on earth pink, yellow and grey. The Blessed Mother said to us: 'Look, dear children, how happy these people are! They lack nothing.'"

Vicka said that she also felt in her heart the immense happiness of these people in heaven. So I asked her,

"I bet you wanted to stay there and never go back to earth." She told me, "Yes, of course, when you see heaven, you have no desire to leave it. It's too, too beautiful! But I knew Our Lady needed me to share her messages with others, so I accepted my return to earth."

Speaking about Heaven, you will be pleased to learn this. When the apparitions began, Ivanka was sad because her mother had died two months before.

The visionary Jakov.
He was 11 in 1982.

Then, on Ivanka's birthday, Our Lady had a gift: she brought Ivanka's mother with her during the apparition. Ivanka said, "I have never seen my mother looking so beautiful."

In the following years, Our Lady came a few more times with Ivanka's mom, and Ivanka said that each time her mother was even more beautiful. Why? Well, God is so great, that in heaven we will never stop discovering him! Therefore, our happiness will keep on increasing as well as our beauty.

Purgatory. Vicka continues the story: "After heaven, the Gospa brought Jakov and me to see purgatory. Now that's a completely different place! It was so foggy that you couldn't even see the people who were there. But you could feel their suffering. You could perceive their moaning, their crying, because they were suffering a great deal. It made a deep impression on us. I'll never be able to forget that place! Our Lady said to us, 'See how much these people are suffering! They are waiting for your prayers so they can go to Heaven. I ask you to pray every day for the souls in purgatory." And when they are in Heaven they pray for us…

Here, I have to explain something. Purgatory is like the waiting room for heaven. It's a temporary place, reserved for those who can't go straight to heaven. What's stopping them? Well, they didn't love Jesus and the other people on earth enough, and they didn't sincerely regret the bad things they did. So they needed a good shower to wash themselves, to purify themselves of their sins. You see, sin dirties the soul, and no sin can enter heaven.

An angel carries a soul to Heaven

But the beautiful thing is that in purgatory the suffering is a suffering of love. Those who find themselves there recognize that they have wounded the heart of God. And since they have finally encountered the love of God at the moment of their death, they love him, and they suffer for having made him suffer so much because of their sins. They're in a hurry to get out of there! And guess what? You can help them with your prayers, just as Mary told Vicka and Jakov! Vicka told me, "If you too had seen purgatory, you would want to empty it completely, to relieve the suffering of these people! You would never forget to pray for these poor souls."

Hell is a place where only those who choose to act against God go. Those who wanted to reject God during their lifetime and right up until their last hour. God loves them and He wants to save them, but He cannot force them to go with Him to Heaven! You can't force love! We all are free to say yes or no to God.

In hell, Vicka saw a huge fire, but a kind of fire that doesn't exist on earth. She saw people throwing themselves into the fire without anyone pushing them. As I told you, they are free! These people were transformed into some grotesque animals of the sort she had never seen before. They were full of hatred and they were cursing God.

When the three visits were finished, Mary said to them, "I have shown you these places so that you would know that they exist and so that you would tell others." She also strongly urged them to "pray for sinners," so that they would feel sorry for their sins, ask forgiveness, and choose to go to Heaven with God.

She also said that there are people on earth (for example, the atheists), who believe that there is nothing after death, that we just disappear forever as if we didn't have souls. How awful! Fortunately, our Heavenly Mother spoke very clearly to the children. "That is a huge error, because after death there is eternity. We are just passengers on earth; when we die, our life goes on." And eternity never ever ends! We will live forever with Jesus in Heaven if we choose to go with Him.

7. Summary of this incredible visit

So to sum it up, each of us has three possibilities after we die: Either we go directly to heaven, or before reaching Heaven we spend some time in purgatory to be cleansed of our sins, or we refuse God right to the end and go to hell, the only place where you can't find God.

I can guess what's going through your minds. "I just hope I go to heaven when I die!" Well, don't worry; you have nothing to fear. If you choose to live with Jesus under the guidance of Mary, God will always be with you and he will guide your steps towards heaven. In your heart, tell Mary that you want to go to heaven, ask her to help you, and she will. Besides that, I have some good news to tell you.

The Blessed Mother said, "Death doesn't exist. Death is simply passing from this life to another life." It's like going from one room to another in the same house. Or even better, it's like going from one corner of the room to another corner of the same room. Now isn't that good news?

In fact, Vicka told me, "If people knew how much God loves them, they would never be afraid of death."

One day, a priest in Medjugorje died. His name was Fr. Slavko. He was a great friend of the Blessed Mother – He let her be known and loved by many people. Mary didn't say to us, "he's dead." No. She said, "he is born into heaven." Do you know why? Because when God

"I am beautiful because I love"

© Bernard Gallagher   "L' Immacolata" of Tihaljina

created us, He didn't create us to remain stuck on earth! No, He created us to live with Him forever. So our real birthday is when we enter heaven. Before that, on earth, we are like infants inside our mother's womb, waiting to be born. And this mother, you can certainly guess, is Our Lady, Our Mother in Heaven.

8. The Beauty of Our Lady

Now, I'd like talk to you about the beauty of the Blessed Virgin Mary. You see, Jakov was just 10 years old at the time of the first apparition. He was the youngest. After the apparition, he was crazy with joy and he told his friends, "The Gospa is the most beautiful woman I've ever seen in my whole life!"

One day he asked her, "Gospa, how is it that you are so beautiful?" She answered, "I am beautiful because I love. There is no one on this earth who doesn't want to be beautiful. So, if you want to be beautiful, love!" Do you want to be beautiful, too? That's normal! Then it's simple, no need for all those beauty products that are so expensive, because with God, it's free! Just make sure that your heart is always full of love; then everyone will notice your beauty.

What is marvelous about the Blessed Mother is that not only is she very beautiful on the outside, but very beautiful on the inside as well. And all the beauty that she has on the inside, in her pure heart, flows out in her eyes, in her smile, in her gestures. That's why the visionaries never want an apparition to end. They feel so wonderful with her!

Often people search for external beauty, but if the heart is full of bad things, what good is beauty? It's just deceptive make-up. When the heart is full of love, even if a person is old, the beauty of their face shines. I'm sure that you, too, want to have this beauty, don't you?

I described to you a little while ago how the Blessed Mother presents herself each day to the children, wearing her grey-blue robe; but I have to make clear an important detail: on Christmas day, she comes with a beautiful robe of gold, resplendent like the sun. She carries the newborn Child Jesus in her arms, and she is surrounded by angels. That is the most joyful day of the whole year. The little Child is wrapped in the golden veil of his mother. At certain times, he sleeps peacefully in her arms. At other times, he has his eyes open and he

A tiny pilgrim

gazes at his Mother with tenderness. But sometimes he turns to the people present in the room and he pauses to look at each person, gently, with amazement, as though he is discovering them for the very first time.

On Christmas day in 1981, guess what? He was playing peek-a-boo behind his Mother's neck! Covering himself up with her veil and then revealing himself, just like a little rascal! I think he wanted to distract the visionaries and make them laugh, because they were still very intimidated and – this is just between us – still pretty uptight. The Child Jesus succeeded in his trick! When the children told me the story, they were still laughing. On that evening, they understood that God is very close to us. We simply need to be ourselves with Him, without acting high and mighty. He loves us as we are.

9. The Gaze of the Mother of God

Jakov explained to me something that is very interesting. During the apparition, he felt the gaze of the Blessed Mother go deep inside of him. He even said to me, ·

Mirjana in ecstasy

"She knows all about me, from my head down to my toes. Nothing is hidden. She sees everything, everything, absolutely everything!" But don't think that it's upsetting, the way it is when someone knows our secrets or even sometimes our sins, the ones we're ashamed of.

Of course, she can see all that is wrong in us, but instead of stopping there and being disgusted as we would perhaps be, her gaze goes further, and she sees with amazement the beauty of the soul. Because our souls were not only created by God but are made in the image of God. They resemble God! Now isn't that a real wonder?

You, for example, don't see the souls of people, but Our Lady does! You can understand now why the gaze of Mary is so encouraging, so loving! It's the tenderness of a mother who reassures us and who keeps us from being afraid along the pathway of life.

One day, she said, "Dear Children, if you saw the tenderness that is found in the heart of every person, you would love everyone the way I love them, even those who seem bad." You see now what a privilege it is to have such a Mother in heaven! What comfort! She's the Mother Jesus gave us. His own Mother, the best of all! When your friends don't understand you or reject you – up you go, jump into her arms! Snuggle up against her heart, and you will feel better!

9 bis The tenderness of Jesus

One day, in the year 1982, Our Lady gave the visionaries an incredible surprise. Not everyone was present, but Vicka recounted the scene for me. She was at her grandparent's house when Mary appeared with her Son Jesus! But not like at Christmas when she is all radiant and holds her little newborn in her arms! No, this time, Jesus was an adult. It was Good Friday. Surely you remember that Good Friday is the day when Jesus died on the Cross.

That day, the visionaries actually saw Jesus appear near his Mother, wearing a crown of thorns. He was suffering his Passion. Blood was running down his forehead, onto his cheeks and into his beard. His face was covered with spit and mud, all swollen from the blows, which he had received during the night in the High Priest's prison and by the cruel abuse of Pilate's soldiers that morning. He was wearing a red cloak that was torn and stained with blood.

To see Jesus in such a terrible state was very hard for the young visionaries because they had never imagined that such agony was possible. It's one thing to know that Jesus suffered for us, but another to see him with your own eyes, real, covered with blood, and as close to you as a member of your own family! Then the Blessed Mother said to them, "Dear children, today I have come with my Son Jesus in his Passion, so that you can see how much he suffered for you and how much he loves you!" So I asked Vicka, "Did Jesus speak to you also?"

She answered, "No, he was silent. He didn't say anything. But I looked at his eyes, and in his eyes I saw such tenderness, such love, such humility, that for me it was more powerful than any word he could have spoken. I saw how much he was suffering and at the same time how much he loved us! You know, I will never forget Jesus' eyes in the midst of his suffering!"

I must admit that this story of Vicka touched me very deeply, because when I am tempted to complain about things of little importance all I have to do is recall that scene and say to myself, "But this is nothing compared to what Jesus endured!" I imagine also the gaze of Jesus resting on me with that immense tenderness, and it makes me surrender completely! How can we resist such a love? It's easy enough to love when everything is going well, but... when one is in agony! How did Jesus manage to continue loving us when he was being assaulted with blows and when he was subjected to the most offensive humiliations? No doubt because he is Love itself! Everything in him is Love! Looking at him makes me love him more and more.

As a matter of fact, I understand better now what happens when someone looks at the suffering of Jesus in this way: Jesus communicates to us his tenderness! His own tenderness enters us little by little like a light rain which gently soaks into the very dry earth. In order to let our own hearts soak it in, we don't have to do anything other than look intently into Jesus' eyes, as Vicka did, because then it is he himself who acts! Let's be still and just let Jesus communicate himself to us directly; then our gaze will become beautiful too.

As for the Blessed Mother, she has already succeeded! She has looked at Jesus with her heart so intensely that she has the same eyes he has! Then she brings him to us so that we can receive the very same gift and resemble him. How lovely!

10. Prayer is so simple!

You must have noticed that often, people don't think about Jesus or Mary. Yes, we forget them! But they never forget us, never! They are with us day and night.

So, naturally Our Lady came to explain to us how to think about them more often, because their presence at our side is truly real! In a certain way, Mary comes to teach us to live each day with her and Jesus, as with our best friends, even if we don't see them with our eyes. And that is called prayer. Prayer is very simple. It is thinking about them and speaking with them in your heart or out loud, being with them the way you are with your best friends.

Suppose that one day there is something which hurts you, why not speak to Jesus about it? You just need to open up your heart to him with this pain. He has also suffered, so he will understand you. If you are happy, thank Jesus! He loves it when you talk to him about your life. Here, I'll give you a beautiful example:

One day in Medjugorje, the "Militia" guards took the six visionaries into a neighboring city, without even telling their parents how long they would be, or where they were going. The parents were really upset, as you can imagine! They asked themselves why people were taking their children, and they imagined the worst! Well, quite simply, the guards wanted to do medical exams of the children and perform special tests. Since they didn't believe in God, they were attempting to

A young man praying during the Youth Festival

prove that the children were crazy and that they were speaking nonsense.

In the evening, the guards brought them back to their village and Our Lady appeared! What joy for the children to find her there again with so much warmth and love, after having been so mistreated all day!

And so, for nearly an hour, they told the Blessed Mother all the details of that horrible experience: how the guards had left them without anything to eat or drink, how they spoke to them in a mean way, how they threatened them, ridiculed them and humiliated them in a thousand ways. Our Lady listened to each tale with a great deal of love.

After an hour, she said to them, "Yes, you are telling the truth. I was there with you. I saw everything, heard everything!" Then the children said to her, "But if you were there and you saw everything, why did you let us tell you all of that, as though you didn't know anything about it?" Now, listen carefully to what Mary said, "Yes, I already knew everything, but for a mother it is such a great joy to hear her child tell all that is in it's heart!"

You see, that remark from our Heavenly Mother already explains quite well what prayer is, I mean "prayer with the heart"! It is so simple that everyone can pray with the heart, because everyone has a heart, a heart capable of loving.

A child in love with Jesus

Pilgrims climbing Podbrdo Hill

11. A Child Who Prays Obtains Wonders!

By the way, that reminds me of an absolutely astounding event which happened to little Jakov.

During an apparition, the Virgin Mary asked him to pray constantly, that is, to remain always open to the presence of God in his heart. She advised him to say little, very short prayers often, when he was going to school, when he was walking down the street or playing with his friends, when he sat down at the dinner table, etc. For example, "Oh, Jesus, I love you!" or "Lord, blessed be your name!" or "Mary, my Mother, help me, I need you!" or "My God, I adore you!" or "Jesus, I place my trust in you!" or "Father, I abandon myself to you." You see, these are little words that come straight from the heart! Jakov understood the advice and decided to put it into practice.

The next day, he had a soccer match with his friends. I have to tell you that Jakov is passionate about soccer. So he got himself ready, ran towards the field, and realized suddenly that he had forgotten to pray along the way. Actually, he hadn't even thought of praying, because he was thinking only about soccer and the fun that was awaiting him. But, since he loved Our Lady so much, he stopped running and very quickly recited a Hail Mary to her before joining the players.

Prayer with the heart

In the evening, when the Blessed Mother appeared to him, she said, "Thank you, Jakov, for the prayer that you offered me, even if you said it very fast." Then, during the apparition, he saw a place in China, a very strange country for him. There, he entered a house and, in one of the rooms, there was a bed. On the bed was a man. Our Lady said to him, "You see this man, Jakov? He's dead. He was a very bad man and he was on his way to Hell. But thanks to your prayer, I was able to help him. By a special grace, he was sorry for his faults at the last minute; and so now he is saved!"

I hardly need to tell you how overwhelmed Jakov was about this. A simple prayer and a man changed his direction for all of eternity! What power there is in prayer! Besides, Our Lady said in a message, "Dear Children, if you only knew the value of the least of your prayers, you would pray without ceasing!"

12. Resisting Evil is possible

You see, our Heavenly Mother knows our talents, and she wants to help us develop them. She sees, for example, that through prayer, we can distance ourselves from evil, conquer evil. So why let ourselves be trapped by Satan, the enemy of God and man, when you can disarm him with a simple prayer?

Suppose you had the temptation to harm someone, or to say something bad about him. That happens to everyone, those kinds of feelings. Of course, you know in your heart that it isn't right, and that God wouldn't like it. So when you come to that realization, don't worry about it. Right away, say a little prayer, "Lord, help me resist this bad idea that I've got running around in my head!" You'll see: that simple prayer will help you have better feelings. Now if the temptation comes back, just repeat the prayer, and there you go, you have conquered!

The Blessed Mother has said, "Dear Children, when you have prayed, you are so much more beautiful!" That's to be expected! When you pray, you attract to yourself all the beautiful treasures that are in the heart of God!

Place of Apparition on Podbrdo Hill

44

13. Don't Forget to Water Your Soul!

I'm not joking! One day the Virgin Mary explained how it works. It's quite simple; you'll see. Take for example a plant that you have in your home, one that you chose at the flower shop, because it was pleasing to you. In the beginning it's rather small, but you know that it's going to grow if you take care of it. Every day you give it a little water, and from day to day, you see it grow new leaves, new flowers. It will show you its beautiful colors.

But if you become lazy to the point where you say to yourself, "Fine, today it can live without water." Too bad! That plant is going to suffer from thirst and it will start losing some of its beauty. The next day, you'll find an excuse not to water it, and you'll neglect it. It will lose some more of its beauty, and the young shoots will stop developing. And if, each day, you leave it without water, it's going to dry up and end up dying.

Well, you see, it's the same thing with prayer. Your soul is like that beautiful plant that God has offered you. It is infinitely precious! He gave it to you, because he trusts you, and he sees in advance the beauty that it is going to develop little by little. So, each day, God gives you his divine grace, just as you give water to your plant. The water, you see, is like grace. It is the gift of God. And to water it is like doing what? It's like praying! Each time you pray with all your heart, you allow God to water your soul with his graces, and he fills it with his treasures! It is all so simple and so beautiful!

Celebration during the Youth Festival

14. With Jesus, You Won't Be Afraid

You must have noticed that some people never pray. Well, we must not judge them, for very often it is because no one has ever really explained to them what prayer is. The problem is that sometimes these people criticize others who do pray. If one of your friends criticizes you, for example, well, don't get into a panic about it. Someone might make fun of you by saying you're wasting your time, or he might tell you things that are hard to hear.

What should you do under these circumstances? Right away, take refuge in your friend Jesus and tell him, "Jesus, please, bless this friend who doesn't believe in you!" Afterwards, you simply avoid useless discussion and you continue to pray calmly, as if you hadn't heard a thing. You see, in life, the important thing is to do things which please God, rather than choose things which please other people. Especially because one day, when that friend sees God face to face at the moment of death, he will understand that he was mistaken in telling you not to pray.

But also, the most incredible thing is that he will be aware of your having prayed for him! He will bless you for it! He will love you immensely, seeing that you, on that particular day, instead of judging him, prayed for him. Because he will see that you have drawn to his soul very precious treasures thanks to your kindness and to your prayer. In a word, he will see clearly what he didn't see while he was still on earth, when he made fun of you.

15. What Awaits Us in Heaven

In Medjugorje, the Blessed Mother explains to us so many useful things for our everyday lives and for the difficult moments we may face. She tells us to think a lot about heaven, because heaven is the real goal of our lives. It wasn't for nothing that she showed heaven to Vicka and Jakov!

Oh, I have to share with you another beautiful thing that she taught us! She told us that in heaven, the elect will see everything in the light of God! There, we will know exactly what each person has done for us on earth. For example, if you say a prayer for a soul that is still suffering in purgatory and if, thanks to your prayer, that soul goes more quickly to heaven, well, that soul will know it, and for all eternity that person will have

Vicka shares
Mary's messages

a very particular love for you! And will pray for you when in Heaven!!!

You see, in heaven, all our secrets will be known! The bad things will be swept away, forgotten, and only the good that we've done will be kept. Nice, huh? And since we never know when the Lord is going to call us back to him, well, it's wise to prepare ourselves for our final journey, starting from today! How do you do that? By always choosing the best for our soul, since our soul will live for ever.

16. Forgiveness Gives us Joy

If you aren't too tired, I really want to tell you another story. This one happened at the beginning of the apparitions, on August 2nd 1981.

One evening, the visionaries were outside, waiting for Our Lady's apparition. A lot of villagers from Medjugorje had come to pray with them, but, of course, those villagers had never seen the Virgin Mary. That evening, a surprise awaited them: Right when she arrived, Mary told them, "This evening, all the people present will be able to come and touch me." The visionaries answered, "But, Gospa, they can't touch you, because they can't see you!" "Yes," she answered, "bring them to me yourselves by the arm, one by one, and they'll be able to touch me." And that is what they did! Each one had the great privilege of touching the Blessed Mother. Imagine!

I know some of these people personally, and they say that it was simply extraordinary to feel under their hands the veil of Our Lady, her head, her arms, etc. They were overcome with joy!

But it happened that after some time, the visionaries noticed that stains were forming on the robe of the Blessed Mother. Weird! Our Lady is always so pure and so impeccable! Dirtiness never reaches her! So the visionaries cried out, "Gospa, what's happening? Your robe is becoming all dirty!" Now listen what she said to them, sadly, "These are the sins of those touching me!

Their hands are dirty with sins!" So the visionaries cried out to the people, "Stop touching the Gospa! You're putting stains on her robe!" The people pulled back, with long faces, quite embarrassed.

That night, Our Lady delivered a beautiful message for the villagers and for all of us: "Dear Children, I invite you to purify your souls from sin. With sin, there is no peace. I invite you to make a confession each month,

Our Lady says "Go to confession once a month"

© Bernard Gallagher

because there is no one on earth who doesn't need monthly confession. Monthly confession will be a remedy for the Church in the West!"

And you know what? From this day on, all the villagers went to confession! You should have seen the results! Wow! There were reconciliations among people. They hugged each other like brothers. They were full of joy! Some were even cured from illnesses.

What can you take from all that? Well, when you have a temptation to do something bad, remember this story. I don't think you would want to add stains to the robe of your dear Mother, would you? Just the opposite! You would choose instead to please her, am I right? And if you ever put some of those stains there (that happens to us all on one day or another), well, quickly, quickly, don't delay. Ask for her forgiveness with all your heart. She will always pardon you! And ask forgiveness from Jesus, too. He is so happy when someone comes back to him with all his heart!

And the message about confession? Hold onto it, because in that beautiful sacrament, it is Jesus who conceals himself in the priest to forgive your sins. Afterwards, you will feel so light, so free, so joyful! The forgiveness of Jesus brings us so much good!

17. The Blue Cross

Before we say goodbye, I want to ask you a question: do you really and truly understand the love of your Mother in heaven? And do you realize how strong she is?

In order to convince you, I would like to let you in on an important story in the lives of our visionaries. Very quickly after the beginning of the apparitions, Our Lady inspired them to form a prayer group. They had gotten into the habit of meeting on the hill of Podbrdo, which overlooked their houses, to play the guitar and pray together. But as you have heard, at that time, atheists were looking for opportunities to harass the visionaries and their friends in different ways.

It was for this reason that the prayer group was always looking for a secret place to pray, in order to hide from the police. Sometimes they would pray in fields or in houses but there was one place at the foot of Podbrdo Hill where they felt safe. This place has a story. One evening, as the prayer group was climbing, Our Lady appeared to Ivan unexpectedly and she warned him to go no further uphill because the Militia guards were waiting for them at the place of the Apparitions in order to catch them. So they stayed where they were; that saved them! Our Lady prayed with them, and from that day on, they would often meet in that secret spot to pray. They felt so safe there!

Later on, a wooden cross was put up on that spot. Ivan had a jar of blue paint at his house, so he painted the cross. That is why, in Medjugorje, everyone calls that place "The Blue Cross."

Now thousands and thousands of people come to pray before this simple blue cross. They recite the rosary or sing hymns or pray in silence. I can't even tell you how many graces are given by God in this place! Sometimes, even now, Our Lady appears to the visionary Mirjana there, on the second day of the month, and many people come to pray around her.

And in the summer time, Ivan the visionary has a prayer group meeting at 10 pm on Mondays and Fridays.

The Blue Cross, place of great miracles

18. You Have a Wonderful Mother in Heaven!

Why am I finishing with this rather unique story of the Blue Cross? Because I want you to keep one thing in mind: You have a marvelous Mother, the Blessed Virgin Mary! Yes, she is yours too! Just as she has helped those young people, this Mother will stretch out her motherly cloak around you –Yes, you, my little friend!!! She will hide you from the eyes of evil people. In this way, she will prevent them from doing you harm or leading you in sinful ways.

Yes, you have a Mother who dreams only about helping you, guiding you, teaching you true things and turning you away from false things; a Mother who looks at you with infinite love, day and night; a Mother who is always ready to console you, to keep you from danger, to protect you! In a word, you have a true Mother, a Mother who will never leave you. A Mother who helps you realize God's plans for you.

But to get the most out of this Mother whom Jesus gives you, on your part, you can also return good for good. Because you see, she has one great desire with regard to you: that you trust her completely! That you pour out your heart to her, telling her in all sincerity,

"Mother, I love you! Thank you for coming to Medjugorje! Today I want to take your hand, so that you will walk with me always. I want to stay with you always, next to your motherly heart. Next to your heart, I will learn to love Jesus,

your Son, and to put into practice the words that he gave us in the Gospel. And Mother, do you know what? I'm sending you a big, big, big kiss right now!"

Vicka's motherly embrace of a child sick with cancer

CD 57min

The Beautiful Story of Medjugorje
as told to children
Sr. Emmanuel

©Childrenofmedjugorje.com 2012

Rejoice! You can also get the CD of this "Beautiful Story of Medjugorje", told by Sr. Emmanuel, with instrumental music played by Roland Patzleiner from Medjugorje.

Distributed in the USA by Children of Medjugorje Inc.

Please visit www.childrenofmedjugorje.com

For distribution in other continents,

See the same website and also

www.enfantsdemedjugorje.fr

Price: 5.00 € in Europe

Other titles by the same author

Books available through the COM website:
www.childrenofmedjugorje.com
or from Queenship Publishing: www.queenship.org
The Amazing Secret of the Souls in Purgatory
Medjugorje, The Triumph of the Heart
Freed and Healed Through Fasting

****

Books distributed by Children of Medjugorje Inc. - USA
www.childrenofmedjugorje.com
comments@childrenofmedjugorje.com
The Hidden Child of Medjugorje
Children, Help My Heart Triumph! (also on E-book)
Maryam of Bethlehem, The Little Arab (also on E-book)
Secrets of Purgatory in The Spotlight (also on E-book)
The Beautiful Story of Medjugorje... (also on E-book)

These titles are available in other countries.
For a list of distributors, please visit
www.childrenofmedjugorje.com
or www.enfantsdemedjugorje.fr

Pray with the young people of Medjugorje!

Consecration to the Heart of Jesus

O Jesus, we know that you are meek, that you have given your heart for us. It was crowned with thorns by our sins. We know that today you still pray for us, so that we will not be lost. Jesus, remember us if we fall into sin. Through your most Sacred Heart, make us all love one another. Cause hatred to disappear among men. Show us your love. All of us love you, and we desire that you protect us with your heart of the Good Shepherd. Enter into each heart Jesus! Knock on the door of our hearts. Be patient and tenacious with us. We are still locked up in ourselves, because we have not understood your will. Knock continuously, O Jesus. Make our hearts open up to you, at least when we remember the passion which you suffered for us. Amen.

Consecration to the Immaculate Heart of Mary

O Immaculate Heart of Mary, overflowing with goodness, show us your love for us. May the flame of your heart, O Mary, descend upon all peoples. We love you immensely. Impress in our hearts a true love. May our hearts yearn for you! O Mary, meek and humble of heart, remember us when we sin. You know that we men are sinners. Through your most sacred and maternal heart, cure us from every spiritual illness. Make us capable of looking at the beauty of your maternal heart, and that, thus we may be converted by the flame of your Heart. Amen.

(Prayers from Our Lady received by Jelena Vasilj in 1983, at Medjugorje)